EMPOWERING THE 21ST CENTURY WORKER

By

Denise N. Fyffe

Empowering the 21st Century Worker
Copyright © 2015, 2021, 2023 by Denise N. Fyffe

All rights reserved.

Published in the United States by Jamaica Pen Publishers. theislandjournal.com/publishing

No part of this publication may be reproduced, stored in a retrieval system, or transmitted in any form or by any means (electronic, photocopying, recording, or otherwise) except with written permission of the publisher and in accordance with the provisions of the Copyright, Designs and Patents Act 1988.

PRINTED IN THE UNITED STATES OF AMERICA

Book design by Jamaica Pen Publishers

Fourth Edition

ISBN: 979-8392302154

Jamaica Pen Publishers

TABLE OF CONTENTS

INTRODUCTION 11

EXAMINING EMPLOYEE EMPOWERMENT 14

   MANAGEMENT THEORIES 15

      Self-determination Theory 17

      Expectancy Theory 19

      Transformational Leadership Theory 21

      Social Exchange Theory 23

   THE BENEFITS OF EMPOWERING WORKERS 26

      Increased Productivity: 26

      Higher Job Satisfaction 27

      Greater Creativity 28

      Improved Employee Retention 28

      Better Decision Making 29

      Increased Innovation 29

      Enhanced Customer Satisfaction 29

      Competitive Advantage 29

   STRATEGIES FOR EMPOWERING WORKERS 31

      Providing Opportunities for Professional Development 31

      Encouraging Open Communication 31

    Creating a Culture of Trust and Collaboration 32

    Defining Roles and Expectations Clearly 32

    Recognizing and Rewarding Employees 33

    Providing a Supportive Work Environment 33

CHALLENGES TO EMPOWERING WORKERS 35

    Resistance to Change 35

    Lack of Resources 36

    Communication Barriers 37

TECHNOLOGY AND EMPLOYEE EMPOWERMENT 39

    Collaboration Tools 39

    Online Learning Platforms 40

    Remote Work Options 41

    Streamlining Processes 41

    Access to Information 42

    Real-time Feedback 42

    Customized Learning 42

EMPOWERING WORKERS: REAL WORLD APPLICATION 45

    CASE STUDY 1: GOOGLE 45

    CASE STUDY 2: ZAPPOS 46

- Case Study 3: Patagonia 47
- Case Study 4: Whole Foods Market 48
- Case Study 5: Buffer 49
- Case Study 6: Basecamp 49
- Case Study 7: Semco 49

THE FUTURE OF EMPLOYEE EMPOWERMENT 51
- Flexibility and Remote Work 51
- Digital Skills 52
- Theory Evolution 53
- Empowering Diversity and Inclusion 53
- AI and Machine Learning 54
- Continuous Learning and Development .. 56
- Social Responsibility and Sustainability .. 56
- Personalization and Customization 57

EMPOWERING WORKERS THROUGH TRAINING AND TECHNOLOGY 59
- Building a Learning Organization 62
- The Pedagogics of Work and Learning 66
- The Adult Learner 70
- The Learning Management System 74

THE LEARNING CONTENT MANAGEMENT SYSTEM 76

IN DEPTH CASE STUDY: HEART TRUST NTA 82

THE PROBLEM 85
THE EXPLORATION 88
THE RESEARCH 90
Interview with Senior Program Director.....98
The Analysis..103
Implications and Recommendations 115
GLOSSARY 120
REFERENCES..124

ABOUT THE AUTHOR 126
RECOMMENDED BOOKS 128
DEAR READER...132

EMPOWERING THE 21ST CENTURY WORKER

INTRODUCTION

In today's modern business landscape, employers must recognize that their responsibility to their employees goes beyond merely providing them with a job. To foster a consistently positive and productive work environment, employers must implement strategies that empower their workers. While some business owners may believe that implementing practices such as open communication, rewards systems, clear role definitions, and accountability alone will ensure employee empowerment, this is not the case.

Employee empowerment involves granting workers the autonomy to make decisions that are not limited to the managerial level. By involving employees in decision-making processes, managers can alleviate stress and increase efficiency in their daily operations. Empowering employees is not just a partial practice, it should be woven into the fabric of an organization's culture and reflected in every aspect of employee policy. Such measures inspire confidence in employees, enabling them to excel and exceed their potential.

Furthermore, investing in accessible training opportunities for employees is a direct and efficient means of empowering them. By providing on-the-job training, employers equip their workers with the knowledge, skills, and attitudes required to perform their job duties effectively. The primary benefit of such a strategy is improved productivity, as employees are best positioned to offer recommendations for enhancing business processes and increasing customer satisfaction rates. Empowered employees attract more customers and offer higher quality services, leading to increased profits.

In this book, we will use qualitative and quantitative methods to explore employee empowerment strategies. We will review the statistical findings of a study conducted on a company's attempt to provide on-the-job training, analyze the short-term outcomes, and provide recommendations based on our findings. By implementing employee empowerment strategies, businesses can cultivate a culture of trust, creativity, and productivity, leading to long-term success..

EXAMINING EMPLOYEE EMPOWERMENT

Employee empowerment refers to the process of providing workers with the tools, resources, and autonomy necessary to make decisions that impact their work. In the 21st century, the concept of employee empowerment has evolved to include a focus on creating a work environment where employees feel valued, engaged, and motivated to contribute to the success of the organization.

The modern workforce is increasingly diverse and dynamic, with employees from different generations, cultures, and backgrounds working together. As such, the concept of employee empowerment has become even more critical in ensuring that all employees feel supported and enabled to succeed.

Employee empowerment also involves recognizing and valuing the unique skills and perspectives that each employee brings to the table. In the 21st century, this means creating a workplace culture that fosters collaboration, innovation, and creativity. It also means providing opportunities for professional development, mentoring, and learning to help employees grow and develop their skills over time.

Overall, employee empowerment in the 21st century is about creating a work environment that supports and enables employees to make meaningful contributions to the organization while feeling valued and engaged in their work.

Management Theories

The concept of employee empowerment is rooted in several management theories, including:

1. Self-determination theory: This theory suggests that people have an innate need for autonomy, competence, and relatedness in their work, and that meeting these needs can lead to greater motivation, well-being, and performance.

2. Expectancy theory: This theory proposes that people are motivated by the belief that their efforts will lead to desired outcomes, and that providing employees with the tools and resources to succeed can increase their motivation and performance.
3. Transformational leadership theory: This theory emphasizes the importance of leaders empowering and inspiring their followers to achieve their full potential and suggests that this can lead to higher levels of engagement, satisfaction, and performance among employees.
4. Social exchange theory: This theory suggests that employees are more likely to be committed to their organizations and work harder when they feel that their contributions are valued and that they are receiving something in return, such as recognition, rewards, or opportunities for growth and development.

These theories can inform strategies for employee empowerment in the 21st century, such as providing training and development opportunities, involving employees in decision-making processes, recognizing and rewarding their contributions, and creating a supportive and inclusive work environment.

Self-determination Theory

Self-determination theory (SDT) proposes that people have an innate need for autonomy, competence, and relatedness, and that these needs must be met for individuals to be motivated, engaged, and satisfied in their work. Autonomy refers to the degree of control individuals have over their work and the decisions they make, while competence refers to the sense of proficiency and effectiveness individuals feel in their work.

Relatedness, on the other hand, refers to the sense of connection and belonging individuals feel with their colleagues and the broader organization. When these needs are met, employees are more likely to be intrinsically motivated, which is associated with greater well-being, job satisfaction, and performance.

To foster employee empowerment in line with SDT, organizations can provide employees with greater autonomy and decision-making authority, such as by allowing them to choose how they perform their work, setting their own goals, or involving them in decision-making processes. Organizations can also provide employees with opportunities for skill development and growth, which can help satisfy their need for competence. Finally, organizations can create a supportive and inclusive work environment that fosters a sense of belonging and connectedness among employees.

An example of Self-Determination Theory in action is the company Zappos, which has been recognized for its employee-focused culture. Zappos provides employees with a great deal of autonomy and decision-making power, allowing them to find meaning and purpose in their work. The company also invests heavily in employee development, providing ongoing training and opportunities for growth. By providing employees with a sense of autonomy, competence, and relatedness, Zappos has created a work environment where employees feel motivated and empowered to do their best work.

Expectancy Theory

Expectancy theory suggests that people are motivated by the belief that their efforts will lead to desired outcomes, and that providing employees with the tools and resources to succeed can increase their motivation and performance. This theory proposes that employees will be more motivated to exert effort when they believe that their efforts will result in high performance, which in turn will lead to desirable outcomes such as rewards or recognition. In order to foster employee empowerment in line with expectancy theory, organizations can ensure that employees have the resources and support they need to succeed, such as providing access to training, technology, and information.

Organizations can also ensure that employees understand how their efforts are linked to desirable outcomes, such as by setting clear performance expectations and goals, and providing feedback and recognition for high performance. Additionally, organizations can provide employees with meaningful and challenging work, which can increase their sense of competence and motivation.

Finally, organizations can foster a culture of empowerment by involving employees in decision-making processes and giving them a voice in how work is performed, and goals are set. By empowering employees in line with expectancy theory, organizations can increase their motivation, engagement, and performance.

An example of Expectancy Theory in action can be seen at Starbucks, which offers its employees a variety of rewards and incentives for meeting performance goals. According to

Expectancy Theory, employees are more likely to be motivated when they believe that their efforts will lead to improved performance, which will in turn lead to desired outcomes (such as a promotion or a bonus). At Starbucks, employees are given clear performance expectations, and they are provided with the necessary training and resources to meet those expectations. They are also offered a range of rewards, such as pay raises, stock options, and opportunities for career advancement, which are tied to their performance. By aligning the performance expectations with the rewards and incentives, Starbucks has created a work environment where employees feel motivated to work hard and achieve their goals.

Transformational Leadership Theory

Transformational leadership theory proposes that leaders can inspire and motivate followers to go beyond their self-interests and work towards a shared vision by creating a sense of purpose, intellectual stimulation, individualized consideration, and idealized influence. Leaders who exhibit these behaviors are able to create a climate of empowerment in which followers are encouraged to take ownership of their work, seek out opportunities for growth, and collaborate with others. Such leaders are also able to create a sense of trust and mutual respect with their followers, which is critical for promoting empowerment.

To foster employee empowerment in line with transformational leadership theory, leaders can create a shared vision that aligns with the values and goals of their followers and communicate this vision in a compelling and inspiring way. Leaders can also provide followers with opportunities to learn and grow, such as through training, mentoring, and job enrichment. Additionally, leaders can provide individualized consideration by showing a genuine interest in their followers' well-being and supporting their personal and professional goals. Finally, leaders can exhibit idealized influence by modeling ethical and values-based behavior and creating a culture of transparency and accountability.

One well-known example of transformational leadership in action is the leadership style of Steve Jobs at Apple. Jobs was known for his charismatic leadership style and ability to inspire his employees to push boundaries and innovate. He encouraged his employees to take risks and think creatively, empowering them to take ownership of their work and make decisions that would drive the success of the company. This leadership approach resulted in Apple becoming one of the most successful and innovative companies in the world.

Social Exchange Theory

Social exchange theory proposes that relationships between individuals are based on the exchange of resources, and that individuals will be more likely to engage in positive behaviors if they believe that their efforts will be reciprocated with rewards or benefits. In the workplace, employees are more likely to be motivated and engaged when they feel that their contributions are valued and recognized by their supervisors and colleagues. This theory suggests that by creating a climate of empowerment, organizations can foster a sense of reciprocity and increase the likelihood that employees will engage in positive behaviors such as going above and beyond their job duties.

To foster employee empowerment in line with social exchange theory, organizations can provide employees with rewards and recognition for their contributions, such as through performance-based bonuses, promotions, or public acknowledgement of their achievements. Organizations can also provide employees with opportunities to give feedback and participate in decision-making processes, which can help employees feel valued and respected. Additionally, organizations can create a culture of collaboration and mutual support, which can foster a sense of reciprocity and encourage employees to help each other succeed. Finally, organizations can create a sense of shared purpose and vision, which can help employees feel invested in the success of the organization and motivated to work towards its goals.

An example of social exchange theory in action can be seen in the workplace when employees receive rewards or recognition for their performance. This could be in the form of a bonus, promotion, or even a simple thank you from a supervisor. In return, the employee may feel a sense of obligation to continue performing well in their job and contributing to the success of the organization. This reciprocal relationship between the employee and the employer creates a positive work environment where both parties benefit from the exchange.

The Benefits of Empowering Workers

Empowering workers has become an increasingly popular management philosophy in the 21st century, with many business owners recognizing the numerous advantages it can offer. The benefits of empowering workers are wide-ranging and can have a significant impact on a company's success. Let us explore some of the most important benefits of empowering workers, including increased productivity, higher job satisfaction, and greater creativity.

Increased Productivity:

One of the most significant benefits of empowering workers is the potential for increased productivity. When employees are given the authority to make decisions and take ownership of their work, they are often more motivated to perform at a higher level. This sense of ownership and responsibility can lead to increased engagement and commitment to the job, which in turn can lead to improved productivity. Additionally, empowered employees are better able to solve problems and make quick decisions, which can help to streamline business processes and increase efficiency.

Higher Job Satisfaction

Empowering workers can also lead to higher levels of job satisfaction. When employees feel that they have a say in how their work is done, they are more likely to feel invested in their jobs and feel like they are making a meaningful contribution. This sense of purpose and ownership can lead to increased job satisfaction, which can have a positive impact on employee retention rates. Additionally, employees who are empowered are more likely to feel valued and respected by their employers, which can further contribute to job satisfaction.

Greater Creativity

Another significant benefit of empowering workers is the potential for greater creativity. When employees are given the freedom to experiment and explore new ideas, they are more likely to produce innovative solutions to problems. Empowered employees are also more likely to take risks and try new approaches, which can lead to breakthroughs in product development, marketing, and other areas. This kind of creativity can be a powerful driver of business success, giving companies a competitive edge in the marketplace.

Improved Employee Retention

Empowered employees tend to be more loyal and committed to their organizations, resulting in lower turnover rates. When workers feel valued and trusted, they are more likely to stay with the company for the long term.

Better Decision Making

Empowering workers provides them with the freedom to make their own decisions and take ownership of their work. As a result, employees are more likely to make informed decisions that benefit the organization as a whole.

Increased Innovation

Empowering workers encourages them to be more creative and think outside the box. This can lead to new ideas and innovative solutions that can improve the organization's products, services, or processes.

Enhanced Customer Satisfaction

Empowered workers are better equipped to address customer needs and concerns quickly and effectively, leading to higher levels of customer satisfaction.

Competitive Advantage

Organizations that empower their workers gain a competitive advantage over those that do not. Empowered employees are more productive, engaged, and motivated, which can lead to higher profits and market share.

Overall, empowering workers can have a significant impact on a company's success, leading to increased productivity, higher job satisfaction, and greater creativity. By giving employees the authority to make decisions and take ownership of their work, businesses can create a more engaged and committed workforce, which can lead to long-term success.

Strategies for Empowering Workers

Empowering workers is a process that requires a deliberate effort by employers to provide their employees with the necessary tools and resources to excel in their roles.

Here are six specific strategies that organizations can use to empower their workers:

Providing Opportunities for Professional Development

One of the most effective ways to empower workers is to provide them with opportunities for professional development. This can include training programs, workshops, mentoring, and coaching sessions. By investing in their employees' development, employers can equip them with the skills and knowledge needed to take on new challenges and responsibilities, boosting their confidence and competence.

Encouraging Open Communication

Open communication is critical for creating an environment where workers feel comfortable sharing their ideas and concerns. Employers can encourage open communication by establishing channels for feedback and creating a culture that values transparency and honesty. This approach helps to build trust between management and employees, which can lead to better collaboration and teamwork.

Creating a Culture of Trust and Collaboration

A culture of trust and collaboration is essential for empowering workers. Employers can create this culture by fostering an environment that encourages open communication, mutual respect, and a willingness to work together to achieve common goals. By creating a culture that values teamwork and collaboration, organizations can empower workers to take ownership of their work and contribute to the company's success.

Defining Roles and Expectations Clearly

Workers need to understand their roles and responsibilities clearly to perform effectively.

Employers can empower their workers by providing them with clear job descriptions and outlining their expectations. This approach helps workers to focus on their responsibilities and prioritize their tasks, resulting in improved productivity and performance.

Recognizing and Rewarding Employees

Recognizing and rewarding employees for their hard work and achievements is critical for empowering workers. Employers can use rewards such as bonuses, promotions, and public recognition to motivate and encourage employees to excel in their roles. This approach not only boosts employee morale but also creates a sense of ownership and pride in their work.

Providing a Supportive Work Environment

A supportive work environment is vital for empowering workers. Employers can provide this by promoting work-life balance, ensuring a safe and healthy workplace, and offering resources for mental health and wellness. By creating a supportive work environment, employers can help workers to feel valued and respected, leading to increased job satisfaction and productivity.

Overall, employers can empower their workers by providing opportunities for professional development, encouraging open communication, creating a culture of trust and collaboration, defining roles and expectations clearly, recognizing and rewarding employees, and providing a supportive work environment. These strategies can help organizations to improve employee engagement, boost productivity, and achieve long-term success.

Challenges to Empowering Workers

Empowering workers can be a daunting task for employers, and there are a variety of challenges that can arise in the process.

Resistance to Change

One of the biggest challenges employers may face when attempting to empower their workers is resistance to change. Employees who are used to a particular way of doing things may be hesitant to embrace new approaches or processes. This resistance can manifest itself in a number of ways, including reluctance to adopt new technologies or methods, pushback against new policies or procedures, or simply a lack of enthusiasm for change.

To overcome this challenge, employers can take steps to communicate the benefits of empowerment to their workers, including how it can lead to increased job satisfaction and greater autonomy. Employers can also involve employees in the process of change, asking for feedback and suggestions for improvement. This can help to create a sense of ownership and investment in the process, making it more likely that employees will embrace new approaches.

Lack of Resources

Another challenge to empowering workers is a lack of resources. Empowering workers may require investments in training, technology, and other resources that employers may not have readily available. This can be especially challenging for small businesses or those operating on tight budgets.

To address this challenge, employers can explore alternative ways of providing training and support to their workers. For example, online training modules or peer-to-peer mentoring programs can provide cost-effective options for professional development. Employers can also consider outsourcing certain functions or processes, allowing them to focus on core competencies while still providing the necessary resources for employee empowerment.

Communication Barriers

Finally, communication barriers can be a significant challenge to empowering workers. Effective communication is critical for ensuring that employees understand their roles and responsibilities, as well as any new policies or procedures that may be implemented. However, communication can be impeded by language barriers, cultural differences, or other factors that may hinder effective communication.

To overcome communication barriers, employers can take steps to promote open communication and transparency within the organization. This may include providing language training for employees who may not speak the primary language of the organization, offering opportunities for cross-cultural exchange and education, and using a variety of communication channels to ensure that messages are received and understood. By breaking down communication barriers, employers can create a culture of collaboration and empowerment that benefits both workers and the organization as a whole.

Technology and Employee Empowerment

The advent of technology has significantly impacted the way businesses operate, and the concept of employee empowerment is no exception. With technological advancements, employers can provide their workers with the necessary tools and resources to enable them to work more autonomously, make independent decisions, and contribute meaningfully to the organization's goals. In this essay, we will explore how technology can be used to empower workers, with a focus on collaboration tools, online learning platforms, and remote work options.

Collaboration Tools

Collaboration tools are software applications that allow individuals to work together on a project or task regardless of their physical location. These tools can take various forms, such as instant messaging platforms, video conferencing tools, and project management software. By providing these tools, employers can empower their workers by allowing them to collaborate in real-time, share ideas, and contribute to the development of the project. Moreover, collaboration tools promote transparency and accountability, as all team members have access to the project's progress and can provide feedback.

Online Learning Platforms

Another way that technology can be used to empower workers is through online learning platforms. These platforms offer employees the opportunity to develop new skills, improve their job performance, and increase their knowledge base. By providing online training opportunities, employers can empower their workers to take charge of their professional development, and in turn, contribute more effectively to the organization. Online learning platforms are also cost-effective, flexible, and can be accessed from anywhere with an internet connection.

Remote Work Options

Remote work, or telecommuting, has become increasingly popular due to advancements in technology. With remote work options, workers can work from anywhere, as long as they have access to a computer and the internet. This provides employees with greater flexibility and autonomy over their work, which can lead to increased productivity and job satisfaction. Additionally, remote work options can reduce commuting time and costs, which can have a positive impact on the environment and workers' well-being.

Streamlining Processes

Technology can be used to automate tasks and processes, which can free up time for workers to focus on higher-value tasks. This can help to increase productivity and job satisfaction.

Access to Information

Technology can provide workers with easy access to information that they need to perform their jobs effectively. This can include everything from product information to customer data. With this information at their fingertips, workers can make informed decisions and provide better service to customers.

Real-time Feedback

Technology can be used to provide workers with real-time feedback on their performance. This can help them to identify areas for improvement and adjust on the fly. This can lead to greater job satisfaction and a sense of empowerment.

Customized Learning

Technology can be used to provide workers with customized learning experiences that are tailored to their individual needs and learning styles. This can help to increase their skills and knowledge, which can lead to greater job satisfaction and a sense of empowerment.

Overall, technology can be a powerful tool for empowering workers. Collaboration tools, online learning platforms, and remote work options are just a few examples of how employers can leverage technology to enable their employees to work more autonomously, make independent decisions, and contribute meaningfully to the organization's goals. By embracing these technologies, employers can create a more empowered and engaged workforce, which can lead to increased productivity, job satisfaction, and overall success for the organization.

EMPOWERING WORKERS: REAL WORLD APPLICATION

Here are a few real-world examples of companies that have successfully empowered their workers. Some of their strategies are highlighted and the benefits they have seen as a result.

Case Study 1: Google

Google is one of the most well-known companies that have successfully implemented a culture of employee empowerment. The company's 20%-time policy allows employees to spend one day a week working on personal projects that align with the company's goals. This strategy not only encourages creativity and innovation but also helps employees develop new skills and interests. Additionally, Google provides its employees with ample opportunities for professional development through regular training and mentorship programs.

As a result of these initiatives, Google has been consistently ranked as one of the best places to work, with high levels of job satisfaction among its employees. The company's commitment to employee empowerment has also led to several breakthrough products and services, such as Google Maps, Google News, and Gmail.

Case Study 2: Zappos

Zappos, an online shoe and clothing retailer, is another company that has successfully empowered its workers. The company's core values, which include "deliver wow through service" and "build a positive team and family spirit," are central to its culture of employee empowerment. Zappos provides its employees with extensive training and development opportunities, including regular coaching sessions and leadership training programs.

The company also encourages open communication and collaboration, with regular town hall meetings and team-building activities. As a result of these initiatives, Zappos has been able to create a strong culture of employee engagement and job satisfaction. In addition, the company has seen significant improvements in customer service and has been recognized for its outstanding workplace culture.

Case Study 3: Patagonia

Patagonia, an outdoor clothing and gear company, is another example of a company that has successfully empowered its workers. The company's mission statement, "Build the best product, cause no unnecessary harm, use business to inspire and implement solutions to the environmental crisis," is central to its culture of employee empowerment. Patagonia provides its employees with opportunities for professional development, such as language classes and leadership training.

In addition, the company encourages its employees to take time off to pursue environmental causes, with a generous environmental internship program. Patagonia has also implemented several eco-friendly initiatives, such as using recycled materials in its products and reducing waste in its supply chain. As a result of these initiatives, Patagonia has been able to attract and retain highly motivated employees and has been recognized for its commitment to sustainability and employee empowerment.

Case Study 4: Whole Foods Market

Whole Foods is a grocery store chain that places a strong emphasis on employee empowerment. They have a "Declaration of Interdependence" that outlines their core values and commitments to their employees, customers, suppliers, and the environment. They also have an open-door policy where employees can voice their concerns or ideas to their managers. Additionally, they offer many training and development programs to help their employees grow and take on new challenges.

Case Study 5: Buffer

This social media management company is known for its transparent and flexible work culture. Employees have the option to work remotely from anywhere in the world, and they are encouraged to take ownership of their work and collaborate with others on their team. Buffer also offers regular feedback and opportunities for growth and development.

Case Study 6: Basecamp

This project management software company believes in giving employees the autonomy to work in the way that suits them best. They have a flat organizational structure, which means that everyone has a say in the decision-making process. Basecamp also encourages employees to take time off when they need it and prioritize their mental health.

Case Study 7: Semco

This Brazilian manufacturing company is known for its unconventional management style.

CEO Ricardo Semler believes in giving employees the freedom to choose their own hours and work from home if they wish. He also encourages employees to take sabbaticals and learn new skills outside of work. As a result, Semco has a highly engaged workforce and has seen significant growth over the years.

These companies demonstrate that there are many different ways to empower workers, and that the benefits can be significant, including increased productivity, job satisfaction, and innovation.

THE FUTURE OF EMPLOYEE EMPOWERMENT

As the workforce continues to evolve in the 21st century, so does the concept of employee empowerment. The future of employee empowerment is set to be shaped by several key trends that are already emerging in the 21st century. Here are some potential future developments in this area:

Flexibility and Remote Work

One of the most significant is the rise of remote work, which has been accelerated by the COVID-19 pandemic. This shift towards remote work is likely to continue, as more and more companies recognize the benefits of flexible work arrangements. By allowing employees to work from home or other locations outside the office, companies can provide their workers with greater autonomy and control over their work schedules, leading to higher levels of job satisfaction and improved work-life balance.

As more employees work from home or other remote locations, companies will need to find new ways to empower them. This could include providing them with the tools and resources they need to work remotely, such as video conferencing software and cloud-based collaboration tools. Companies may also need to create new policies and procedures to ensure that remote workers are able to stay connected and productive.

Digital Skills

Another trend that is likely to impact the future of employee empowerment is the increasing importance of digital skills. As companies become more reliant on technology, it will be essential for workers to possess the skills and knowledge necessary to effectively use digital tools and platforms. This trend is already evident in the growing demand for workers with coding and data analysis skills, as well as in the rise of online learning platforms that allow employees to develop new skills and stay up to date with the latest technological advancements.

Theory Evolution

In addition to these trends, the future of employee empowerment will also be shaped by the continued evolution of leadership theories and management practices. As new research emerges on the most effective ways to empower workers, companies will need to adapt their leadership styles and organizational structures to create more collaborative and participatory work environments. This will require a focus on building trust and transparency within organizations, as well as on fostering open communication and creating opportunities for employee involvement in decision-making processes.

Empowering Diversity and Inclusion

The future of employee empowerment will also be influenced by the growing importance of diversity, equity, and inclusion in the workplace. As companies recognize the value of diverse perspectives and experiences, they will need to create more inclusive cultures that support the needs and interests of all employees. This will require a focus on promoting diversity and inclusion in hiring and promotion practices, as well as on providing support and resources for underrepresented groups.

Companies will need to focus on creating a culture of respect and inclusion, providing support and resources for employees from diverse backgrounds, and empowering employees to take action to promote diversity and inclusion within the company. By creating a more diverse and inclusive workplace, companies can empower all of their employees to reach their full potential and contribute to the company's success.

AI and Machine Learning

Finally, the future of employee empowerment is likely to be shaped by the increasing use of artificial intelligence and other advanced technologies. While these technologies have the potential to automate many tasks and processes, they also have the potential to create new opportunities for workers to take on more challenging and fulfilling roles. To maximize the benefits of these technologies, companies will need to invest in training and development programs that help workers develop the skills and knowledge necessary to effectively use and leverage AI and other advanced tools.

As AI and machine learning continue to advance, companies will be able to use these tools to empower workers in new ways. For example, AI-powered chatbots could be used to provide employees with instant access to information and resources, allowing them to make more informed decisions and work more efficiently. Machine learning algorithms could also be used to analyze employee data and identify patterns that can help companies create more effective employee empowerment programs.

Continuous Learning and Development

As the pace of change continues to accelerate in the business world, companies will need to provide their employees with ongoing learning and development opportunities. This could include offering access to online courses and training programs, as well as encouraging employees to attend conferences and other events that can help them stay up to date with the latest trends and best practices in their field. By investing in their employees' professional development, companies can help them become more empowered and more effective in their roles.

Social Responsibility and Sustainability

As consumers become more socially conscious, companies will need to prioritize social responsibility and sustainability in their business practices. This includes empowering employees to make a positive impact on their communities and the environment. For example, companies could encourage their employees to volunteer in their local communities or provide them with opportunities to participate in sustainability initiatives within the company.

Personalization and Customization

As technology continues to advance, companies will be able to provide more personalized and customized experiences for their employees. This could include tailoring employee empowerment programs to each individual employee's needs and preferences, or using data analytics to identify areas where each employee could benefit from additional support or training. By providing personalized and customized experiences, companies can help employees feel more empowered and engaged in their work.

Overall, the future of employee empowerment is set to be shaped by a range of trends, from the rise of remote work to the increasing importance of digital skills and diversity, equity, and inclusion. To create truly empowered workforces, companies will need to adapt their leadership styles, organizational structures, and technological infrastructures to support the needs and interests of their employees. By doing so, they can create more collaborative, productive, and fulfilling work environments that benefit both employees and organizations alike.

EMPOWERING WORKERS THROUGH TRAINING AND TECHNOLOGY

With the rising trend in adult continuing education many countries, in particular, companies are seeking economical yet effective methods of training. Online and web-based training is the solution. Evans (2000), in his article, **Workers in the new economy: Organization for Economic Cooperation and Development,** posits "... technological changes affecting economies and societies, ... generated new forms of production and exchange, and created new forms of work, but the new economy has not begun to remove the old economy's social problems." The rationale of his article was to explain the role of unions in the new global economy and to highlight how "very much a part of the solution to re-linking growth and the social progress." He believes, "only with them would social problems of the old economy begin to be solved."

The writer states that there is a challenge in bridging the social and digital divide between people who have modern technologies versus those having none. The inequality, he believes, may be reflected in the overwhelming number of workers below the poverty line. Furthermore, the article highlights that there is greater usage of gadgets with emphasis on computing, but this does not ensure prosperity unless people have the necessities including education. Evans (2000) also sees the most successful new age countries as those with organizations balancing the market pressures of adaptation and dynamism with social concerns and dignity of workers. He goes further to state that it is an important priority of the government to invest in education and training, to raise the level and quality of employment.

Workgroups are now seeking union representation as reflected in the increase of union membership in both North America and the United Kingdom. Unions are instruments that counterbalance the forces created by technological changes and globalization, through redressing imbalances of power and ensuring that productivity increases are used to raise the standard of living. Unions have provided computers and low-cost internet as the new way to train and retrain workers and give practical meaning to the term lifelong learning.

Research by the Organization for Economic Cooperation and Development (OECD), states that unions have played a role in the increase of the amount of training done by firms, and this has spread on a wide scale. Firms that have unions are innovative and have raised productivity. An added role along with being negotiators is that of providers, of opportunity to study to Post Graduate levels. The writer supports his main arguments with examples and especially that of a Public Sector Union, UNISON, in the United Kingdom and there over 40 educators have played a significant role of being providers (Evans, 2000).

Building a Learning Organization

In the US, unions are instrumental in ensuring that the use of learning applications is properly utilized by an organization to increase production, worker output, and overall job satisfactoriness. On this basis, Garvin (1993) then defines "learning organization as institutions skilled at creating, acquiring and transferring knowledge and at modifying its behaviour to reflect new knowledge and insights." The article **<u>Building a Learning Organization,</u>** authored by Garvin (1993), illustrates five actions of learning organizations, namely systematic problem solving, experimentation, learning from own experience and history, learning from others' practices and experiences, and filtering knowledge quickly and efficiently.

According to Garvin (1993), this method of systematic problem solving has its foundation on the philosophy and methods of quality movement and relies on scientific methods versus guesswork. It incorporates simple statistical tools such as histograms, charts, and cause and effect diagrams. The second method of experimentation with new approaches is a system where one searches for and tests new knowledge using ongoing programs and demonstration projects.

Another action depicted by Learning Organizations is 'learning from their own experience and history.' In this regard, Garvin (1993) expresses that companies should review success and failure and assess them systematically. These lessons should be recorded and be open and accessible to all. Learning from others' practices and experiences, is the fourth indicator, he established that managers know that different companies can produce fertile sources of ideas and catalysts for creative thinking; hence they steal ideas shamelessly (SIS) better known as Benchmarking.

Filtering knowledge quickly and efficiently throughout organizations is one sure way to become a learning organization. This way knowledge would spread quickly and efficiently throughout the organization. Mediums such as reports, tours, and personnel rotation are utilized to facilitate this process. Whatever the source of outside ideas, learning would only occur in a receptive environment. Learning organizations by contrast cultivate the art of open attentive listening.

The use of illustrations and examples provided by Garvin is excellent in facilitating the understanding of how the above-mentioned actions are implemented in organizations and how they 'bear fruit.' They are on point and are clear in illustrating how these companies have sustained themselves and expanded over the decades. However, it leaves one to question the continued use of large co-operations, as examples, such as Xerox, General Electric, Boeing, and NUMMI. He has not mentioned smaller businesses. The question remains whether there are any organizations of a different category that may employ these actions.

Because of the actions implemented, learning organizations can then be measured by the Cognitive *(members exposed to new ideas and to think differently)*, Behavioural *(internalize new insights and alter behaviour)* and Performance Improvement *(measurable improvements and performance)* categories. Improvement can be seen in the tangible gains of superior quality of production, better delivery, and an increase in market share.

Garvin's main views were that learning organizations are not built overnight. There must be the first step to foster an environment conducive to learning and learning is different when employees are harmed or pressured. He also states that training in brainstorming, problem-solving, evaluating experiments, and other core learning skills are essential, and boundaries should be opened to stimulate new ideas.

Garvin's points are integral and fundamental to the topic as it generates many questions. The article also generates new ideas and a better understanding of how systems and policies are implemented. It gives rise to the necessity of consideration and discussion being supported by employee participation. This leads to Spencer's article which refers to the relationship of organizations and employees, the consequences, and benefits for both if opinions are voiced and considered from the employee by the organization.

The Pedagogics of Work and Learning

Bruce Spencer (2002) in his article, **Research and the pedagogics of work and learning** argues that workforce learning is a problematic activity that may not result in the celebration of employee empowerment and autonomy. He claims the opposite, stating that the entrenchment of existing power relations is the norm. Moreover, the article puts forward that workplace learning refers to the education that takes place at work daily. It extends the idea of a learning organization to include a concept of collective "learning that results from individual learning, arguing that organizations must foster and support such learning to remain competitive." Presented, as a 'win-win' situation is the idea that individuals develop as organizations grow, and as organizations decide to encourage greater decision-making, workers choose to complete their tasks, and teams are encouraged to foster workplace democracy.

There is an underlying tension, between work and learning, which has been overlooked. Overall, the article contends that the projected enthusiasm for 'lifelong learning, learning society and learning organization' has blunted researchers' scrutiny as to what occurs in the workplace (Spencer, 2002). Also, instead of all the 'rosy-eyed promises and changes which are to occur in the place of work, the opposite is likely to take place. If this negative change does occur then the danger, of which Spencer emphasizes of "equally brave new world of pedagogics concerning 'work and learning' would become part of the new forms of oppression and control in the workplace."

The article demonstrates how empowered workers, who challenge policies within the organizations, are quickly silenced and relegated to conform to the social relations of the workplace. Learning Organizations are adept at hiding their reassertion of employer rights and control in the workplace as part of the new form of oppression. People are always learning in the workplace, whether to take orders or to conduct the job in a less stressful or exhaustive way. It is said that workers who enjoy greater job satisfaction have a larger role in the decision-making process, which is often linked to the technical quality of the job.

These workers who are trained by the organization are of some worry to them (the organization), as they are "trying to benefit from granting educational opportunities to their employees" and hope they do not leave to work for another organization. Hence, organizations favour their budgets for professional workers, and less is earmarked for those who have "little or no formal training" (Spencer, 2002). The article also ties in the role of unions as Evans did in his article, **Workers in the new economy: Organization for Economic Cooperation and Development.** However, Spencer dictated that "in addition unions and workers may also want to ensure that there is equity in all training and educational provision, which is not too employer-specific, that workers can enjoy some paid educational leave and that the increased knowledge would benefit workers financially."

Spencer's article covered many other writings and these writings and illustrations unlike that of Evans (2000) were in the late nineties. He fundamentally tied in strategic areas such as workplace learning, society, education, facilitating learning, and the role of adult educators. Though intrinsic in its contribution to the phenomenon of workplace learning, this article is overly robust and not easily digested mentally. Time must be spent to absorb the information.

In closing, it refers to the importance of adult educators in an organization, and their acceptance of the workplace being a location of learning. In living up to being learning organizations as defined by Garvin (1993), these organizations have joined forces with adult educators and even refer to them as consultants. Spencer (2002), in quoting Peruniak (1998), states that "they have accepted competency-based training as a norm and have welcomed employer-determined curriculum." Spencer accepts lifelong learning as benefiting workers and employers, so does Jarvis (2003), who shares and emphasizes the importance of Adult Learning and the continuation of this process throughout one's lifespan.

The Adult Learner

Jarvis (2003), in his book **Adult & Continuing Education: Theory and Practice,** summarises adult learning "as a lifelong process which has acquired greater significance as the speed of change in society has increased forcing members to." continue "learning to remain members." He argues that lifelong learning is different from lifelong education and maintains that education should be provided for people throughout their lives but not exclusively by the state.

To clarify further, Knowles (1998) in his book, **The Adult Learner: The Definitive Classic in Adult Education and Human Resource Development,** defines education as, "an activity undertaken or initiated by one or more agents that are designed to effect changes in the knowledge, skill, and attitudes of individuals." This definition emphasizes the educator as a change agent who presents stimuli and reinforcement for learning having designed activities inducing change. Knowles (1998) continues to clarify, by quoting Boyd et al. (1980), that "learning is the act or process by which behavioural change, knowledge, skills, and attitudes are acquired" (pp.100-101). Education, according to Jarvis (2003) is utilized for varying purposes; chief of which is preparation for responding to social change and transmission of culture. This, in an effort not to become alienated from the culture engulfing them as the newer knowledge they learn, the more they remain in harmony with their culture.

Furthermore, Jarvis (2003), quoting Scheler (1980) identifies that some forms of knowledge alter faster than others, which he refers to as artificial because it is the form of knowledge that does not persist over time. An example of this is technological knowledge. He continues to state that there are seven types of knowledge which include myth and legend, religious knowledge, basic types of metaphysical knowledge, philosophical-metaphysical knowledge, positive knowledge of mathematics, natural and cultural sciences, and technological knowledge. "The more technologically based the society, the easier it is for individuals to become alienated," a phenomenon even more prevalent in the arena of employment with many occupations being based upon technological knowledge.

Many professional bodies now encourage and require their employees to undertake regular courses of continuing education and professional development (Jarvis, 2003, Ch. 1). Countless persons do not have the time afforded to study or to acquire skills at formal educational institutions; yet they aspire to fulfil what Maslow refers to as 'the need to know' on his hierarchy of needs; hence, the use of online applications. These same online applications are explained and referred to by Dobbs (2002) and Oakes (2002). Jarvis (2003) has suggested that "human beings have a basic need to learn, and that they are lifelong learners and the provision of education across the lifespan is one way by which people can satisfy this basic need".

Investigating learning is frequently valuable to policy-level executives, managers, and employees as it provides information that would improve decision-making and enviable experiences. With the increased emphasis and growth in technology, it becomes paramount that these persons research and select the most appropriate system for their organization. Consonant with this Dobbs (2002) mentions that in choosing an appropriate system consideration needs to be given to in-house information technology capabilities return on investment, customization needs, and the various models and vendors. He posits that the Learning Management System (LMS) is a vehicle used to automate the administration of online training programs." It is used to track users and courses, record data on student's progress, and forward reports to management — work otherwise conducted by onsite trainers.

The Learning Management System

In the article, **Take the gamble out of an LMS,** Dobbs (2002), explains what the Learning Management System is while giving practical examples of companies using these systems. It also offers insights into various ideas to consider when choosing a Learning Management System and the benefits to respective organizations. LMS is often a multi-year deal hence dealer should be around for the duration and the entire organization needs to be united if the LMS is to be successful (sharing the same objectives). The article advises that management ensure that the LMS is needed and ensuring IT infrastructure can facilitate the implementation of the LMS

Kendle, a pharmaceutical company that needed to scale back on training without compromising quality turned to the emerging technology of the LMS. The writer stated that this was an expensive tool but if the right one is chosen there is the possibility of saving vast amounts of money while advancing workforce development (cognitive, behavioural, and performance capacities of workers). This process is by no means without a degree of difficulty. However, these are the same goals that have been highlighted and explained by Garvin (1993) in providing clarification about learning organizations.

According to Dobbs (2002), quoting James Lundy, an e-learning analyst with Gartner, by the year 2005, 70% of large organizations would be using or own LMS applications. He projects within three years the market would top ME $33 billion. Along with the LMS is the "freshest concept to hit e-learning" (Oakes, 2002) known as the Learning Content Management System, which requires the same due diligence and foresight.

The Learning Content Management System

Oakes (2002) in his article, **LCMS, LMS— They're not just acronyms but powerful systems for learning** seeks to explain why LCMS is not a silly acronym but the freshest concept to hit e-learning since LMS became dominant in the 2000s. The Learning Content Management System (LCMS) is all about the content and providing that content to the user more efficiently and more dynamically. It stands for which as defined by

DC, a system used to create, store, assemble and deliver personalized e-learning content in the form of learning objects.

The term personalize refers to the specification to user needs which are determined by the user's background, level of knowledge in subject matter, job role, and personal preference. E-learning — refers to content delivered electronically, and a learning object is a self-contained chunk of learning that accomplishes a specific learning objective. LCMS should have the right mix, according to Oakes (2002), of the following features. These are authoring and content creation capabilities, support for a wide variety of content formats, robust model for creating and managing learning objects, a scalable object repository (database), good search and browse capabilities, ability to personalize the delivery of content, and a detailed tracking and reporting capabilities.

The Learning Content Management System (LCMS) has not eliminated the need for the

Learning Management System (LMS). An LCMS is content-focused — it tackles the challenges of creating, reusing, managing, and delivering content, whereby the LMS is learner and organization-focused. LMS is concerned with the coordination of managing learners, learning objectives, and the competency of mapping an organization. It lets learners keep track of individual skills and competencies, helps locate and register learners for relevant learning activities, and helps administrators manage and track the relationship between the users.

According to Oakes (2002) a powerful combination for a robust e-learning platform. For this to be successful, they ought to integrate effectively in at least two areas — personalized delivery and tracking. Both Dobbs (2002) and Oakes (2002) have provided clear explanations on the Learning Content Management System (LCMS) and the Learning Management System (LMS). They have set definitions, clarification, and explanations on the purpose and use of the systems. Additionally, they have also ideally highlighted the concept of 'no man stands alone,' implying that the joining of both systems, allows them to be more effective together than apart. These authors have addressed the issues which face organizations considering the purpose, use, and function of these systems. The points are clear and easily understood. However, they also provide guidelines to be carefully followed when selecting them. Chiefly, the benefits are extremely attractive, and the billions of dollars and efficiency inherited is a major benefit for any cooperation's overall productivity and job satisfactoriness.

All the writers mentioned above contribute chiefly to the understanding and investigation into employee empowerment. Their ideas tie in intricately; from the understanding of learning organizations and the role of unions to the importance and understanding of adult education and its relevance. Then the use of online applications is highlighted as they are being employed in the learning organizations to facilitate adult learning.

Each article brings added purpose to the investigation and their main points can stand alone but also intertwine with the others. Some lead to unanswered questions while others provide the basis or foundation for these questions. Overall, these writers have performed a principal and essential function. That is, to provide a firm foundation and to expand upon the context and background of these evaluation efforts.

Furthermore, their works help to further define the concepts of learning, learning organizations, and learning systems – and their purpose. Additionally, they provide an empirical basis for the subsequent development of the theories proposed. Incorporating these works provided much-needed knowledge and understanding while stimulating new ideas. Ideas that demonstrate a familiarity with the body of knowledge gained and its established credibility in the study, included in this text.

IN-DEPTH CASE STUDY: HEART TRUST NTA

Over 18 years ago, I worked with the implementation team at the Heart Trust NTA in Jamaica. This is the national training agency in Jamaica which is fully government-funded by the three percent tax. The decision was made to conduct a parallel run of the new LMS and the old student management system, TIMS, at that time. This was to be conducted over several months. I joined the team as the system administrator and would work to customize the features to match the existing processes at the Vocational Training and Development Institute (VTDI) – the tertiary arm of Heart Trust.

The LMS was designed specifically for the agency and the programmers were on hand to resolve any issues with the coding or alter the framework. This proved helpful as each day was a learning experience. First, we rolled out the student management component, with the Registry team. That meant manually inputting thousands of student records, staff information, setting up user access and rights, along with building out that location's portal.

It was laborious, thrilling, and intrinsically rewarding to be a part of such an endeavor. The parallel run was successful, and the system proved more than capable of replicating the processes, making the Registry more efficient at retrieving records and student information and lessening the time to do all these tasks. After a year, the decision was made to implement the LMS for the additional 30 Vocational Training Centers (VTCs) and Academies across the island. This too was successful after two to three years.

Meanwhile, I continued supporting VTDI and every semester over 100 students and new faculty required training and support. Also, the content management features were, at that time, being implemented to establish online learning classes, for all these students each semester. This was an even greater challenge. Nonetheless, the system supported those requirements for a few years.

However, there was an obstacle preventing 100% usage among the staff. This was a perplexing issue because millions of dollars were spent to design, build, implement and support the system and its users. Careful analysis and planning were done for years before it was even implemented. So, what aspect could have been overlooked to impede such a massive undertaking which by every means should have overcome any hurdles; especially with the design and programming team being fully in-house? The one element that was not accounted for was the human element.

Human beings can overcome, adapt, and find alternatives to almost any new situation. However, human beings can also be the greatest obstacle, especially if they have decided to reject something. When this happens, everything must be done to examine the situation. Then identify what factors are causing the resistance, seek solutions and reach a compromise. A plan needs to be devised to move forward.

The Problem

The LMS was an online application that managed student information for the institution and provided an online portal to create online classes. This would allow students to access their teachers, learning materials, course content, interact via discussions and online chat, complete assignments, and tests. While the student management component was highly effective and made the Registry more efficient, the content management component proved doubly difficult for staff members. Transitioning from the old ways of working, while lacking 21st century skills added on to their workload.

Users were continually complaining and bitterly frustrated with the system, especially the faculty. Complaints pointed out the incapacity to handle and juggle curriculum development, classroom management, assessment, administrative, professional development and every other miscellaneous duty assigned. To add learning a new system to the list, which should make their job easier, but was not, was unacceptable. Have you ever tried convincing over two dozen master's degree and PhDs holding professionals, to do something they do not want to? Then to also do this every day for several weeks? As a newly minted IT professional it was like David vs. Goliath. It is hard to convince someone when they have decided concretely they would not.

Initially, the implementation team thought this was simply resistance to change and tried to implement measures based on that assumption. I adjusted my schedule and approach for training. I switched to conducting one on one sessions with the lecturers. However, I was still met with more complaints, delay tactics, doubts, philosophical suppositions, and every other resistance strategy imaginable. Even though the overall objective was to continue implementing the system at that time, I decided to go back to the drawing board and assess the issue more closely.

I began to listen carefully and changed my perspective to that of the users. The general complaint and resistance stemmed from the system user interface design. Most of the complaints were that the system was not user-friendly. Furthermore, upon closer observation, most of the lecturers who were required to use the system were averse to technology, lacked the requisite digital skills, and additional responsibilities.

The administrative and registry personnel were more open and flexible, no matter the system errors and glitches presented. User feedback was favorable and stated that the system took them from the dark ages to the technological era. It made lighter work. Conversely, the implementation of the LMS and accompanying training only added much more to the already packed list for the lecturers. Understanding their dilemma became paramount in my mind.

The Exploration

I started to explore certain ideas and questions, which arose as to why the implementation and overall acceptance of the system were so difficult and whether workers were brought 'into the loop' about the use, purpose, and cooperative decisions when implementing the system. Were they included in the previous discussions? Were their job responsibilities considered? Those who covertly rejected the system made the implementation process continuously stressful and tedious. Furthermore, millions of taxpayers' dollars were on the line. Also, the success of the implementation and use of the system was jeopardized. So, how could a compromise be reached? What was needed to get the process moving forward and accomplish the over company objectives?

Managers and staff were all required to use the LMS to perform various job tasks, such as storing student biodata, producing registration numbers and reports. The directive was given that the institution would utilize the system for its reporting purposes. Various meetings were held to continually report, assess, and adjust the implementation rollout across the locations. Directors, managers, and other key stakeholders were therefore required to use them on a day-to-day basis in keeping with the directive. Additionally, reports, student administration, and other fundamental processes were directed through the system, to make them easier to manage. It was believed the LMS would make it easier to track a student throughout his lifelong learning at any of the organization's locations.

I learned quickly that staff members were not necessarily sensitive to the overall objective of the organization. Their focus was at the micro-level. THEM. Nonetheless, the implementation of the system was important to the organization's new direction and resources would be wasted if it were not implemented promptly. The implications ranged from a decline in worker productivity, lower levels of job satisfaction and job satisfactoriness, the psychological well-being of the employee, and the growth of the organization as a learning organization. This organization invested millions of dollars in sourcing and developing the system and infrastructure. People were being trained to make it successful. One may be tempted to assume that the system was the problem; however, there may be underlying issues, which I aim to discover.

The Research

To truly derive objective reasoning, information, and solutions, I decided to research from the perspective of employee empowerment. Doing so would provide us with vital information that was unbiased. Certainly, the findings and information gathered should prove useful for other future system implementation – not only with LMS or LCMS. Noteworthy is the fact that in Jamaica and globally, circa 2003, organizations were moving towards using online applications to guide and conduct online classes for students and online training for their staff as well as to streamline and manage increasingly other processes. Overall technology inclusion was the trend for all areas in the business and professional world. Therefore, it was imperative and advantageous to understand and even study these trends and other related factors.

The research aim was to explore the true reasons and purpose for implementing the Learning Management System (LMS) at Heart Trust NTA. To start, I conducted a qualitative exploration so that any resulting determinations or proposals would be based on scholarly references and the ideologies of industry experts. A full understanding was necessary from all angles. Other employees and by extension the productivity of the organization was affected by the overall psychological rejection of the system and the implications of such were far-reaching. If these problems were present, then the company would be impeded and unable to grow and contribute to its basic purpose.

Within that dilemma, it was also imperative to investigate further and determine whether employees were receiving on-the-job training. Further, but more significantly, if they were empowered to have received this training or not. Additionally, it needed to be identified whether workers were satisfied with their job and the training received.

The overall question being posited was 'the extent to which on-the-job training influences the empowerment of workers.' From this primary question, other sub-questions were derived in hopes of gaining a better understanding of the issues experienced during the LMS implementation or highlighting the problem. Some of these questions were:

- Are employees being trained on the job at the respective campus?
- What does the training lead to?
- Is the employee more productive after receiving the training?

- How satisfied are the employees with this training?
- Do the employees believe the training is a cover for increased workload, preparation for promotions, or academic interest only?

One limitation encountered was the unavailability of surplus participants. It became increasingly difficult to find persons who were willing to participate in the research. The target population was the staff members of the institution. This included faculty, administrative and technical staff. Therefore, it took a long time to collect the necessary data from the participants.

In the effort to conduct this study, I utilized methodological triangulation, the process of mixing qualitative and quantitative 'methods' to sourcing data. I chose this approach simply to make the study more comprehensive resulting from the complementary nature of the methods. Questionnaires were administered giving rise to the quantitative analysis while interviews (both formal and informal) were conducted giving credence to the qualitative method. Both methods are present with limitations such as the idea that qualitative research requires more time, greater clarity of goals and results cannot be analyzed by computer programs – hence subjected to the researcher's opinions. Critics argue that quantitative research is too rigid, following a linear path, testing hypotheses linked to casual explanations (Nueman, 2003). It is hoped that utilizing both methods would combat the limitations of the other.

To effectively appropriate the quantitative aspect of the research, questionnaires were administered. These questionnaires were subdivided into three sections – Section A; Section B; Section C. The purpose of the study along with reasonable identification was printed on the top front half of each questionnaire. Instructions on how to complete the instrument were also given in this area. It should be noted that the instructions were emboldened with a larger font size to ensure clarity of understanding.

Questionnaires can utilize close or open-ended questions; however, for this purpose, I chose closed-ended questions. About the short duration of time, I had to complete the research, it was more practical and logical to utilize this method. Close-ended questions "are quicker and easier for both respondents and researchers."

There were other benefits to utilizing this method. Firstly, it would be easier to compare the different answers given and the coding of the answer and statistical analysis would be less problematic. The responses given on the questionnaire would clarify any question not understood. Participants would also be more willing to participate and there would be fewer irrelevant and confusing answers to the questions. The closed-ended questions would rule out the disadvantage, which would have been present for less articulate respondents. Hence utilizing the language that a 13-year-old could understand.

I must admit that there are disadvantages in using only closed-ended questions, and as a safeguard, I utilized open-ended questions for the interview – the other instrument. Use of these questions aided in the rapport-building stage between the researcher and interviewee or respondent. It allowed me to probe the respondent's thinking and ensure he understood the questions, helping the accuracy of the research. However, most importantly it allowed for an unlimited number of responses, and these can be in detail and can be qualified and/or clarified (Neuman, 2000).

To capture more data, a telephone interview was conducted with the Senior Programs Director, at the time, as extenuating circumstances prevented us from meeting face-to-face. The senior director was very gracious and extended himself to provide as much cooperation and assistance as was required. Having already developed a rapport with this gentleman and due to the fact, the researcher had specific questions in mind; the interview was indeed productive to the study. His contribution lent itself to the research by providing another perspective to 'the extent to which on-the-job training influences the empowerment of workers.'

I analyzed the data gathered by first collating all questionnaires received and reflecting the responses in Excel spreadsheets. These responses were grouped, in their respective sections, showing the actual response. The response to a respective question was tabulated and statistically grouped to give percentages and values in some cases while noting similarities and or differences. Responses from the Likert scale were counted, having been grouped in a table, from which percentages were derived.

The interview was taken on its merit. Furthermore, the information gathered in this process was correlated with that collected from the questionnaires. Moreover, the previous qualitative data collection is the foundation of the research. Hence references were continually made to this data. It helped with either contradicting or agreeing with the problem statement.

Interview with Senior Program Director

1. *Is this tertiary institution a Learning Organization?*

Yes. Every day the organization and I promote lifelong learning and this tie into the concept and the commitment to skillset and improvement of the employees. Persons must have job aspirations and are provided with formal training or coaching. Persons must aspire. There is job rotation. (He refers to his experience where he has rotated in various positions and is now the Senior Programs Director). I must embrace technology, hence LMS. TIMS was not robust enough and LMS allows this tracking of the lifelong learning process, to track persons. You take an individual from Level one (1) training to Level five (5), so you can track the individual throughout their learning experience. (He then refers to the New Business Model).

The LMS supports the idea of a Learning Organization (L.O.). There is an idea that I react to the environment and the LMS is a reaction. This enables me to manage the training of more persons and the economic changes in the economy. Training and Certification are provided. As you know we went to Australia and looked at their (LMS) system and patterned the system from them (benchmarking). (He mentions the performance objective system and that this also ties in with the L.O.)

2. *What does the training receive, on the job, leads to? (Increase in salary, workload, promotion, etc.)*

The HR department is producing competencies working towards a skill set. This is developed based on the skill set. The Leadership Development program facilitates the competency that the TVET managers should have over 6 months. (He mentions that he is also involved with a program whose goal is to train and equip managers with the relevant skills to conduct their job.) This program is for different managers, which leads them towards competency-based training. It leads the person from the start to where they should be at the end. Some would receive certification, while for others we would look at the previous training they have received and provide certification.

3. *Does on-the-job training lead to more workload?*

I am going to be guarded about my answer. It can. However, it also leads to a change in schedule, if aiming for another position at a higher level, for example, in management. As managers, you work through people and the tasks get harder. So, on-the-job training does lead to more workload. It is a sacrifice to gain competency.

4. *After receiving on-the-job training are there opportunities for advancement?*

Yes. As you know, there are job postings that go out from time to time. I try to get people to exhibit these competencies. Persons can be pulled from various areas at any time. For example, there is Ms. GM who was put in charge of Skill Jamaica.

There are opportunities from time to time that one might not be paid for. It provides opportunities for workers to demonstrate the institution's core values. (There are seven (7) core values, and a handbook is distributed to employees. There was even a competition on these values).

5. *Does on-the-job training lead to worker empowerment?*

In most cases, yes; if you equip someone with new skills, yes. (He refers to his experience that 4 years ago he did not have his master's degree and he became bored with his position and needed challenges. Once he got his Masters, his mind started to operate at a higher level, and was able to deal with the challenges. He gained more responsibility, and because of that more levels of exposure.)

I feel empowered, as you get to utilize your knowledge and skills and you want to display it. For example, the Enterprise Based department was demotivated and unsure of its role. Once the goals and objectives were explained, seminars were done, trainers and assessors were brought in. This resulted in a cohesive band of persons; they have changed as they have been given the tools. So, on-the-job training empowers persons to perform.

I explained to him that I was pursuing my Career Development and Counselling degree at the time and how the concern or research topic came about and then explained the lack of acceptance for the LMS. He mentioned that they had discovered that the sensitization of the various institutions was not conducted properly. So, persons just viewed this as the IT department pushing on them 'another software' and therefore rejected it. After they had gone, met, and spoken to them then the attitude changed, and persons dealt with the system differently.

I mentioned the issue of explaining the goals and objectives; that for some, the purpose of training is given, but others are just commanded to go and then they wonder why they are there.

He agreed that there are cases where this does occur and others where the goals are clearly explained. I thanked him for his time and the opportunity to interview him.

The Analysis

The findings and especially the results provided more clarity to helped us understand the Agency's goal or objective for employee empowerment. The data was represented in percentages to demonstrate and document, clearly, various patterns and observations. The responses and observations from the interview are also combined and findings were interwoven in the proceeding report.

Most of the participants were educated beyond the Tertiary level with some possessing postgraduate qualifications. They indicated the use of an important technological tool – the computer – weekly for at least an average of 25 hours. These support Evans (2000), as he states in "***Workers in the new economy: Organization for*** *economic cooperation and development*", that there is a greater emphasis on computing with greater usage of gadgets. While acknowledging such sentiments it is important to remember that the Director also indicated that this would not ensure prosperity unless people have the necessities including education. I, therefore, sought to find out whether the sampled population participated in on-the-job training, to which an overwhelming 70% indicated they did. A significant 30% however were not so involved.

Evans continued in the article to posit that it is an important priority of governments to invest in education and training to raise the level and quality of employment. When asked the kind of training the respondents participated in or received, a majority indicated it had to do with computer skills, online applications, and leadership development.

Bruce Spencer (2002) argues that workforce learning is a problematic activity that may result in the celebration of employee empowerment and autonomy, stating that the entrenchment of existing power relations is the norm. The article puts forward that workplace learning refers to the education that takes place at work daily. It extends the idea of a learning organization to include a concept of "collective learning that results from individual learning, arguing that organizations must foster and support such learning to remain competitive."

Presented, as a 'win-win' situation, is the idea that individuals develop as organizations grow, and as organizations decide to encourage greater decision-making, workers choose to complete their tasks, and teams are encouraged to foster workplace democracy. The sampled population would, in the estimation, factor into Spencer's (2002) argument as they indicated personal academic interest as the main reason behind their participation in the job training being conducted. The Senior Programs Director mentioned, in his interview, that the organization along with himself continually promotes lifelong learning with an emphasis on employee improvement.

Jarvis (2003) states that 'many professional bodies now encourage and require their employees to undertake regular courses of continuing education and professional development. These practices, as indicated below by the reference made to the Leadership Development Program and many other courses, enhance worker performance and skill set, is conducted by the institution.

Jarvis (2003) has also suggested that "human beings have a basic need to learn, and that they are lifelong learners and the provision of education across the lifespan is one way by which people can satisfy this basic need". Hence, the various levels of training provided and the usage of the online application the Learning Management System to track users throughout their learning career.

The learning organization provides training for its employees who are potentially earmarked to transcend into future leadership roles. This program, as mentioned by the Senior Programs Director is the Leadership Development Program. This ties in with the argument posited in Spencer's article where he pointed out that companies train their professional workers and hope they do not move on to another organization. To combat this, they are the recipients of handsome packages and other worker benefits. A salary increase was one of the other reasons put forward for such participation. He indicated that persons are often certified for the job training received which do not have financial benefits attached. It was highlighted that these allowed the employee to demonstrate the institution's core values.

The research also explored whether the company communicates its training goals and strategies. According to Garvin (1993), one of the characteristics of a learning organization is the transference of knowledge and the modification of behavior to reflect this new knowledge and behavior. He sees the learning organization as 'institutions skilled at creating, acquiring and filtering knowledge quickly and efficiently.' 43% of the sampled population agreed that the company communicates its training goals and strategies, while 30% disagreed and a further 23% were not sure whether to agree or to disagree when this question was posed to them.

On the question 'opportunities available for me to develop new skills,' 73% agreed that there were opportunities available. The Senior Programs Director reasoned the institution created the LMS as a reaction to the changes in the economy thus making available opportunities for skill development. This could be representative of Garvin's (1993) views that learning organizations were not built overnight. He posits fostering an environment conducive to learning where training in brainstorming, problem-solving, evaluating experiments, and other core learning skills can be developed.

When asked what on-the-job training was associated with, 20% of the respondents believed it led to an increase in workload. The Director mentioned that with training, there is usually an increase in the employee's workload as protocol dictates such. Spencer (2002) asserts that learning organizations are adept at hiding the true meaning of on-the-job training, citing the ease with which workers who challenge policies are quickly silenced. He points out that workers always learn on-the-job even if it is to take orders or to complete newly assigned tasks in less stressful or exhaustive ways.

The Director reinforced that there are adequate opportunities for workers to practice the skills and training received on the job. He made special reference to one manager who was put in charge of a special project because she possessed the necessary tools required to conduct the job having been trained while on the job. The research shows that 67% of the sampled population agreed to some level that they were able to attain the opportunity of using what is learned on the job. This ties in with the statement on the questionnaire that required users to indicate their agreement with the ease of applying this training they had received.

Reflecting on the extent to which on-the-job training influences the empowerment of the worker, the Director cites the case of the Enterprise Based Training (EBT) department whose staff was demotivated and unsure of their role. He stated that the goals and objectives of the department were communicated to the staff, trainers and assessors brought in and training conducted.

He now sees a cohesive band of persons more challenged to complete their assigned tasks, since they were given the tools to facilitate the same. He concludes that the organization empowers persons to apply what they learn to their job areas or duties. Garvin (1993) reiterates this point when he wrote "that time would be doubly productive if employees possess the skills" and were "given boundaries to stimulate their ideas".

Online applications are important to the future success of any organization that seeks to cut costs and increase productivity while empowering its workers to excel in their job. Based on the research, 67% of the respondents utilize the computer to facilitate their day-to-day activities. This is integral because the primary focus of HEART Trust is to access and drive the management aspect of their business.

Jarvis (2003), quoting Scheler (1980) puts forward "the more technologically based the society, the easier it is for individuals to become alienated," a phenomenon even more prevalent in the arena of employment with many occupations being based upon technological knowledge. With this learning organization, emphasis was placed on online applications to facilitate access and steer the management aspect of their business; it became paramount to pose the question 'Considering everything, how satisfied are you with your job?' 53% were satisfied, 17% expressed dissatisfaction, with 30% stating they did not know whether they were satisfied or dissatisfied.

This is further reflected by the Director's rhetoric that having communicated to employees the importance of their respective assignments, they reacted differently with changed attitudes. Garvin (1993) states employees must feel the benefits of the training programs effectively making their jobs more manageable. This I believe is borne out by the results obtained – 53% satisfaction with 30% on the periphery of satisfaction.

Spencer (2002) refers to the importance of adult educators and the acceptance of the workplace as being a location of learning, while accepting that workforce or lifelong learning benefits employees. This is like Jarvis' (2003) argument that workforce learning has increased acquiring greater significance. For the question 'Considering everything, how satisfied are you with your job,' a significant 53% indicated they were, while 30% sat on were indecisive.

The Director highlights his empowerment and satisfaction as a worker when he indicated that at one point in time, he felt overwhelmed and unproductive. He believes that with the training he received on the job, he was more challenged to perform as his mind now operated at a higher level. He mentioned that he was facilitated by the Heart Trust who rotated him in various positions within the institution. Now, this keeps in line with Garvin's (1993) article "***Building a learning organization***". He points out several characteristics of a learning organization, one being 'rotation of personnel to facilitate the filtering of knowledge quickly and efficiently.'

The learning organization included in our study distributes performance objectives for all its full-time employees. These objectives are made up of different tasks to be completed and successfully conducted during the year. Garvin (1993) further illustrates three indicators used to measure a Learning Organization. Employees are exposed to new ideas to alter behavior while improving performance. This begs the question, 'I feel more productive as a worker after receiving on-the-job training,' there was a split of 50% agreeing while 13% disagreed. 23% were not sure how to respond and they were guarded with their responses to protect their jobs.

Spencer (2002) highlights such when he spoke of consequences and or benefits when employees voice opinions separate from the employers.' He believes workplaces and indeed the learning organizations are quite adept at control, effectively silencing dissenting employees. The Director stated this was not entirely representative of the sentiments of the campus as other employees are regularly reassigned based on on-the-job training received as the need arises.

Overall, the data collected is satisfactory. Most of the questions were easily interpreted. Having analyzed the data it becomes apparent that only a generalized estimation can be provided on the level of worker empowerment occurring at this learning organization. Respondents were reluctant to respond to questions for fear and uncertainty of the outcomes of doing so; despite assurances that they would not be personally identified.

Nonetheless, approximately 50% half of the sampled population agreed that they are satisfied on some level with the training they have received on the job, with a further 23% undecided. The researcher estimates that these are representative of the 53% who indicated satisfaction with their job task and assignment at the chosen location.

Implications and Recommendations

Based on the quantitative and qualitative research findings several implications and recommendations can be made about the extent to which on-the-job training influences the empowerment of workers at this learning organization.

Recommendations being pro-offered:

- Communicate the opportunities derived from on-the-job training.
- From the statistics, more persons were satisfied than those very satisfied with their jobs or training received on the job. Create room for improvement in these areas.
- Initiatives, steps, goals, and objectives of the organization should be communicated to all parties involved.
- Create avenues for persons to practice what is learned on-the-job for satisfactoriness to improve.
- Implement initiatives that are not overbearing and allow the employee to feel that they can provide feedback without consequences.

The opportunities which are associated with on-the-job training should be communicated to the employees. This would facilitate the training process and the reception of the training by employees. It is integral that these persons understand the goals and objectives of the company so that they may play their part in the advancement of the institution and not be a detractor of it.

From the statistics, more persons were satisfied than those very satisfied with their jobs or training received on the job. There is always room for improvement in this area. 53% of the persons canvassed were satisfied; measures can be taken to bring the remaining 47% into some level of satisfaction. A satisfied worker is a productive worker and as highlighted in the first recommendations goals should be made clear, but not only so, these goals when accomplished should have equally clear and attainable rewards. The procedures implemented to clarify or attain these goals should not be arduous or laboring to the employee.

Initiatives, steps, goals, and objectives of the organization should be communicated to the parties involved. Not just the initiatives towards on-the-job training but also every aspect and dealings of Heart Trust/NTA. If this measure has already been taken, then it needs to be adhered to and made more visible at the location.

Create avenues for persons to practice what is learned on-the-job for satisfactoriness to improve. If workers are of the opinion that on-the-job training brings in additional work volume and no opportunity to practice or exercise what is learned, then it may be the reflexive action to shun it. However, if there were opportunities presented for the worker to practice what is learned then this would promote job satisfaction and satisfactoriness.

Further research can be conducted on several areas. One main area of interest is the direct reasons to the satisfaction, or lack thereof, of the employee regarding his/her job after the training is received. Another section for further research is the options identified for pursuing on-the-job training. Are these areas relevant? How effective is the training? As several persons indicated that there was insufficient time to practice what is learned from these training, the focus could be drawn to provide further information on this area.

Having been an employee at the learning organization featured in this study, whether purposely or inadvertently, there may be scopes of insight that may be shed on the research findings. Certainly, the data helped to inform the design and implementation of the training strategies conducted thereafter. Being mindful of employee's workload and responsibilities, as well as incorporating them more in the decisions for the training helped greatly to alleviate the stress experienced.

GLOSSARY

- **Administrative Procedures** – management of actions taken during the research process.
- **Adult learning** - "as a lifelong process which has acquired greater significance as the speed of change in society has increased forcing members to..." continue ". . . learning to remain members."
- **Benchmarking** - stealing ideas shamelessly (SIS) better known as Learning from others' practices and experiences.
- **Data** – numerical and non-numerical forms of information collected.
- **Data Analysis** - detailed examination of numerical o non-numerical information collected.
- **Education** - an activity undertaken or initiated by one or more agents that are designed to effect changes in the knowledge, skill, and attitudes of individuals Knowles (1998).
- **Empowerment** – make or become authoritative of one's affairs.

- **Interview Schedule**- a name given to survey instrument when a telephone or face-to-face interview is conducted.
- **Learning Content Management System** - (Oakes, 2002) a system used to create, store, assemble, and deliver personalized e-learning content in the form of learning objects.
- **Learning Management System** - a vehicle used to automate the administration of online training programs." It is used to track users and courses, record data on student's progress, and forward reports to management — work otherwise conducted by onsite trainers.
- **Learning Organization** - learning organizations as institutions skilled at creating, acquiring, and transferring knowledge and at modifying their behavior to reflect new knowledge and insights.
- **Likert Scale** – scale used in survey research where attitudes or feelings are represented on a continuum in ordinal-level categories.

- **Methodological Triangulation** -, the process of mixing qualitative and quantitative 'methods' to sourcing data.
- **Methodology** – any number of systematic procedures used in research.
- **Population** - the name given to the large general group from which the sample is derived.
- **Qualitative Research** – assessing the quality of 'things' using words, images, and worded descriptions.
- **Quantitative Research** - referring to counts and measures of 'things.'
- **Reliability** – consistency, and dependability of the measure of a variable.
- **Research Design** – plan or purpose of the systematic collection and analysis of data.
- **Sample** – set of persons selected from the population to represent the larger pool and generalized to the population.
- **Statistic** – numerical estimate of a population parameter computed from a sample.

- **Validity** – the ability to generalize findings outside a study.
- **Variable** – a concept or its measure that can take on multiple values.

REFERENCES

1. Berg, B. (2004). Qualitative research methods for the social sciences (5th Ed.). Boston, Allyn, and Bacon.
2. Dobbie, K. (2002). Take the gamble out of an LMS: learning management systems are used to automate the administration of online training programs. Retrieved from http://www.findarticles.com/p/articles/mi_m0FXS/is_11_81/ai_94638435
3. Evans, J. (2000). Workers in the new economy: Organization for Economic Cooperation and Development. The OECD Observer, Retrieved from http://www.findarticles.cornlp/articles/mi ga3648
4. Garvin, D. (1993). Building a Learning Organization. Harvard Business Review 78 – 91.
5. Jarvis, P. (2003). Adult & Continuing Education: Theory and Practice (2nd Ed.). RoutledgeFalmer.

6. Knowles, M., Holton III, E., & Swanson, R. (1998). The Adult Learner: The Definitive Classic in Adult Education and Human Resource Development (5th Ed.) Butterworth Heinemann.
7. Neuman, W. (1999). Social Research Methods; Qualitative and Quantitative Approaches (4th Ed.). Boston, Allyn, and Bacon.
8. Neuman, W. (2003). Social Research Methods; Qualitative and Quantitative Approaches (5th Ed.). Boston, Allyn and Bacon.
9. Oakes, K. (2002). LCMS, LMS — They're not just acronyms but powerful systems for learning - E-Learning - learning content management system. Retrieved from http://www.findarticles.com/p/articles/mi_m0MNT/is_3_56/ai_84184612
10. Spencer, B. (2002). Research and the pedagogics of work and learning. Journal of Workplace Learning, Vol. 14 (pp. 298 – 304).

ABOUT THE AUTHOR

Denise N. Fyffe, (DSE, B.Sc., PGDE, M.Ed.) b.1981 from Kingston, Jamaica. For 20 years, she has worked in Education, Training, and with Learning Management Systems (LMS, LCMS). Fyffe collaborated on multiple projects internationally to implement learning management systems and e-learning training programs. She has developed online training curriculum for major companies in the United States.

During her career, she partnered with several organizations including Infoserv Institute of Technology, Heart Trust NTA,

Pearson Education, University College of the Caribbean, and Prometric.

In addition to studying Software Development and Design offered from the Caribbean Institute of Technology, she completed her Bachelor of Science degree in Career Development and Counselling at the Vocational Training and Development Institute. Presently, she holds a Post Graduate Diploma in Education and is pursuing a Master of Education degree. As a child, she attended Harbour View Primary and Camperdown High.

For over 15 years, Fyffe has authored more than 50 books. They range from poetry, fiction and non-fiction. She is a prolific researcher and writer. She holds fast to the philosophy that you should follow your interests; knowledge empowers you. Do not set limitations on your potential.

RECOMMENDED BOOKS

All books are available at online bookstores, including Amazon.com.

Dear Reader

Thank you for reading this book.

It means so much that you have taken di time out of your busy schedule. Nothing makes us happier than knowing that someone is reading, and hopefully enjoying, what took us many months, even years, to create.

Please stay with us on this journey. We welcome your feedback, opinions, and suggestions about di book. We would appreciate a few lines of review on di website where you purchased this book, or on Amazon.

You can also write us a note at our website Jamaica Pen Publishing on Facebook, or Twitter or contact us at any of our social media accounts.

www.ingramcontent.com/pod-product-compliance
Lightning Source LLC
Chambersburg PA
CBHW020431220526
45464CB00002B/660

9798392302154